The Little Captain
and the Pirate Treasure

First published under the title *De kleine kapitein en de schat van Schrik en Vreze*

First published in Great Britain 1980

Printed in Great Britain by
Biddles Ltd, Guildford, Surrey for J.M.Dent & Sons Ltd
Aldine House, Welbeck Street, London
This book is set in 11 on 15½pt Quadritek Baskerville

British Library Cataloguing in Publication Data
Beigel, Paul
The little captain and the pirate treasure
I Title II Hollander, Carl
839.3'1'36J PZ7.B475

ISBN 0-460-06906-3

The Little Captain and the Pirate Treasure

Paul Biegel

illustrated by CARL HOLLANDER
translated by PATRICIA CRAMPTON

J.M. Dent and Sons Ltd
London Toronto Melbourne

Contents

Prologue

which tells you how it all began

The *Neversink* is a very small boat, with an upturned bath-tub for a boiler, a stove-pipe for a furnace and six bottomless buckets for a funnel. Her captain is a small boy in a big cap and he is joined in his adventures by three more children: Marinka, podgy Plum and timid Thomas.

On their first voyage together they rescued six shipwrecked sailors, dealt with tyrants and performed seven hard labours in the land of Nonsense and Knowledge.

Finally, on Tangleroot Island, they met the pirate Scurvyboots and managed to take possession of the seven treasure chests he had stolen, leaving him to sail the seas for ever, his hands clamped to the wheel by magic as a punishment for his wickedness, until someone could find the true owners of the treasure and return it to them . . .

The Pirate Treasure

The *Neversink* was lying in harbour and the little Captain was sitting in the cabin. No fire burned under the boiler, no smoke was coming out of the six-bucket funnel, there was no one on deck, there was no one in the hold. The little Captain was completely alone on his silent boat.

The little Captain was reading.

He was reading an old, crumpled, yellowed piece of paper which he had found in one of the seven treasure chests he had seized from the pirate Scurvyboots on his last voyage.

The little Captain wanted to return the seven chests honestly.

Not to the pirate, of course, because he had stolen them from someone. But from whom? To whom did the treasure really belong?

The little Captain scratched his head under his cap, and he read the old, yellowed, crumpled piece of paper through once more: 'To the great lord of Fear and Terror', it said, and underneath that:

'Herewith the seven chests. Each one is
filled with treasure: crystal bunnies,
copper, silver, rubies red,
diamonds, bigger than your head.
The sixth oak chest is filled with gold,
but luck is what the seventh holds.
I send them to you, sir, by sea,
and as for theft, rely on me!
A thieving hand would, through my spell,
be clamped for ever to the wheel.'

Under these lines there was a jumble of noughts and crosses and lines and dots. They were the writer's signature, but the little Captain could not read it.

'Who could that be?' thought the little Captain. 'And who is the great lord of Fear and Terror?' That was where the treasure had to go, he realized, but who was he, and how was the little Captain to find out where the lord lived?

He took off his cap to help him think, but put it on again at once, because he heard footsteps on the deck and a captain must look neat and tidy when he has visitors.

The visitor was old Salty.

'Well, little Captain,' said old Salty. 'What are you going to do with the seven chests?'

hollander

'Give them back,' said the little Captain.

'Yes, but to whom?' asked old Salty.

The little Captain gave him the old, yellowed and crumpled piece of paper and old Salty began to read. Old Salty read it through three times, sucking so hard on his pipe that the cabin was filled with blue smoke.

'Well, well,' he muttered at last, 'that fits.'

'What fits?' asked the little Captain.

'The signature,' said old Salty, 'it's the signature of a wizard. He's the one who sent the chests off long ago, across the sea, and then Scurvyboots stole them. Ha ha! And as a punishment he's stuck to his ship for good now.'

The little Captain nodded.

'So the chests,' murmured old Salty, 'were on their way to the great lord of Fear and Terror. That's where you're going to take them, is it?'

The little Captain nodded. 'They were meant for him,' he said.

Old Salty nodded too. 'Yes,' he said, 'the great lord of Fear and Terror. Hm! Don't go there, little Captain.'

'What?' cried the little Captain. 'Do you know who he is? Do you know where he lives? Do you know where I can find him ?'

'Sure as ninepence,' said old Salty, 'sure as ninepence. But you mustn't go there, my boy, because the great lord of Fear and Terror lives in the Misty East. And you won't get your ship into any harbour in the Misty East. They have copper cannon and they sink anything strange with their copper cannon.'

'Oh,' said the little Captain. 'But they can't sink the *Neversink*.'

'That's what you think, my boy,' said old Salty.

'That's what I *know*,' said the little Captain.

Old Salty was silent.

'I would like to save Scurvyboots, too,' said the little Captain.

'When I have returned the treasure he will be released from the bewitched wheel.'

Old Salty was silent.

'I shall leave tomorrow,' said the little Captain, 'for the Misty East.'

Then old Salty took off his cap. 'I knew it,' he said quietly, 'I knew you would go, after all, little Captain. Shall I help you load the chests?'

'Thank you,' said the little Captain.

The chests were still standing on the quay and there were a great many people standing round them, and inquisitive children too.

'Can we help?' asked Marinka.

'Much too heavy for girls,' cried podgy Plum.

'This one doesn't weigh anything!' cried Marinka. She shook one of the chests to and fro. 'Ha ha, this one's empty!' she jeered.

That was the seventh chest.

'Keep off!' cried old Salty. 'There's good luck in that one.'

Timid Thomas was there too. Timid Thomas didn't help, but he opened his eyes wide when he heard about the seventh chest.

Night had already fallen before the job was done.

'I shall sail tomorrow morning,' said the little Captain, 'before sunrise. . . !'

On The Way

When the first cock began to crow in the little port between the dunes, it was joined by another sound: a trumpet.

Ta-ran-ta-ra! It sounded in the clear morning air: the copper trumpet of the little Captain. The *Neversink* was about to set sail.

The little boat, laden with seven chests full of treasure, lay deep in the water, but when the little Captain slipped her moorings, echoing footsteps resounded on the quayside.

'Hi, stop!' called two voices. 'Little Captain! Wait a minute, we're coming too!'

She came tripping along like a butterfly — Marinka — and like a butterfly she sprang on deck.

'Oh,' said the little Captain. 'But I'm going a long, long way. To the Misty East.'

'I know,' said Marinka. 'We've brought everything with us.'

She pointed to podgy Plum, who was coming round the corner, puffing like a steam engine. He was carrying a suitcase, a bag, a flour sack, a frying-pan, a telescope, a spare pair of trousers and a fishing rod. And every few seconds one of these things fell to the ground so that every few seconds podgy Plum had to stoop to pick it up again.

'Get moving, slow-coach!' cried Marinka.

'Yes but . . .' the little Captain began.

'No "yes buts",' said Marinka. 'You've got to have someone to bake the pancakes and someone to blow up the fire, haven't you?'

'Well, yes,' said the little Captain, 'but . . .'

'And we're on holiday,' said Marinka.

Podgy Plum stepped aboard.

Marinka was already tugging at the steam whistle.

The little Captain took his place behind the wheel.

'Boiler ten degrees atmospheric pressure!' cried podgy Plum, blowing the flames higher still.

'Batter stirring!' cried Marinka from the galley, cracking an extra egg into it.

'Full steam ahead!' cried the little Captain, standing steady at the helm, feet apart, eyes fixed on the harbour entrance. So began the voyage of the gallant little boat *Neversink* to the Misty East. In the hold were the seven chests filled with treasure which had to be taken to the great lord of Fear and Terror.

'Oh, never mind,' said Marinka. 'Of course he'll be just a nice man and perhaps he'll let us keep something, something gold, you know, because we're bringing it back so honestly.'

The little Captain was silent. He was thinking about the copper cannons.

'Well,' said podgy Plum, 'if he isn't nice, we'll just sail away. He won't get anything. We'll keep it all for ourselves. We'll be nice and rich.'

The little Captain shook his head. 'What about Scurvy-boots?' he asked. 'He would never be released if we did that.'

Marinka did not think that was too terrible. 'That nasty pirate,' she said. 'Come and have a look, Podge,' she said, 'see what's in the treasure chests, see how rich we're going to be?'

'Keep away from them!' cried the little Captain, but the two children had already slipped through the hatch into the hold and the little Captain was left standing thoughtfully behind the wheel.

The sea was rocking gently, the wind was whispering sweet words, as if it could never get angry, and the air was as blue as a peacock's neck.

'Hey!' came podgy Plum's voice as his head appeared through the hatch. 'Hey, little Captain, there's an animal in one of the chests.'

'Have you looked inside, then?' asked the little Captain.

'No,' said podgy Plum. 'We can hear it. We can hear it scrabbling and yammering and sighing.'

The little Captain switched off the engine and fixed the wheel

hollander

and followed podgy Plum into the hold.

Marinka was standing by the chest. It was the seventh chest. Seven sighs came from it.

'Must be a tiger,' said Marinka.

But it was not a tiger.

As the lid slowly opened a crack, a pale little face appeared and a thin little voice asked: 'Am I in Lollipop Land at last?'

It was timid Thomas.

'Deck-swabber!' cried Marinka. 'How did you get in there?'

'You made a fool of me!' moaned Thomas. 'It's not a lucky chest at all. It's an unlucky chest. Look where I've got to now!'

'On to the *Neversink*,' said the little Captain.

'And I didn't want to go to sea!' wailed timid Thomas.

'Doesn't matter,' said Marinka comfortingly. 'We'll be landing again very soon. And then you can go and visit the great lord of Fear and Terror.'

'Wh-wh-who, wh-wh-what? I want to go home!' whined timid Thomas, quaking.

'Then in you dive and swim back!' cried podgy Plum.

But it was much too far. The blue sea lay round about them, the home port was out of sight and the *Neversink* steamed on, on her way to the Misty East.

Sobbing, timid Thomas swabbed the deck.

Singing, Marinka baked pancakes.

Panting, podgy Plum blew up the fire under the boiler. And while the little Captain stood steering and peering, he was thinking to himself: 'Odd, that, the seventh chest, the lucky chest, quite empty . . . or is timid Thomas the luck . . ?'

Brave Marinka

The *Neversink* had already sailed across three blue seas and put in to thirteen ports: Siliku and Proosht and Cali . . . but we don't have to name them all. Each port lay closer to the Misty East and in each port the people knew more about the Misty East.

'Don't go there,' said the old salts on the quays.

'You can only land at night, when the moon is down,' said the smugglers in the pubs.

'They'll blow your brains out,' said the old sea lawyers on the park benches.

The little Captain nodded at whatever they said. 'I know,' he said, 'with copper cannons.'

'C-c-copper c-cannons?' chattered timid Thomas whenever he heard them. 'I want to go home!'

But Marinka bought flour for the pancakes, podgy Plum bought coal for the furnace under the boiler and the little Captain bought charts in order to find the way. And then they sailed on, to the place where the sun rises like a red ball from the waves every morning, to the east, the Misty East.

And one day they saw it lying there, far ahead on the horizon. Tall blue mountains, with green palm trees and white palaces, and under them a row, and then another row, and yet another row of glittering lights.

They were the sun's rays flashing from the copper cannons. They had just been polished. 'They're going to fire!' cried timid Thomas, fleeing for the hold.

'You go and sit in the lucky chest,' cried Marinka. 'They won't catch you there.'

But the *Neversink* was still too far off to be fired on and the little Captain lowered the anchor.

'The lucky chest,' he muttered thoughtfully. 'That's an idea!'

'What do you mean, little Captain?' asked Marinka.

Then the little Captain told them his plan. He said: 'If the great lord of Fear and Terror knew we were bringing treasure he would not let the copper cannons fire on the *Neversink*.'

'No,' said podgy Plum. 'That's obvious. But he doesn't know.'

'And so,' said the little Captain, 'one of us must go ashore to tell him.'

'Ashore?' asked podgy Plum. 'How? Swim?'

'No,' said the little Captain. 'In the lucky chest.'

'Aha!' cried podgy Plum. 'Timid Thomas!'

'No,' said the little Captain. 'Timid Thomas is too timid.'

'Well,' said podgy Plum. 'I'm too fat. I would sink, chest and all. You go, little Captain.'

But Marinka, who had heard everything, cried: 'Oh no, a

captain always stays with his ship!' And then Marinka said: 'I'll go.'

She was a brave Marinka.

The little Captain doffed his cap to her and said: 'Marinka, the lucky chest will drift into harbour on the tide. That will give you an hour. Then it will be ebb tide and it must bring the chest back again. We'll be waiting for you here.'

'Right,' said Marinka. 'An hour is enough. The great lord of Fear and Terror will be glad to hear about the treasure. I don't need to be afraid of him.'

She turned and went into the cabin. There she put on her prettiest butterfly dress, tied three red ribbons in her long hair and reappeared garbed like a princess.

Timid Thomas had to help lower the chest into the water.

'Goodbye Shivershanks,' said Marinka, and leaping like a butterfly over the railing, she was in the chest in one bound.

'Just like a little wooden house on the water!' called Marinka. 'Shut the lid and shove off!' A moment later the chest was bobbing slowly into port on the waves of the incoming tide. The lid was slightly ajar, as an air-hole, and as a peep-hole for brave Marinka.

Three little figures stood staring after her over the bows of the *Neversink*.

'Lucky chest,' murmured the little Captain. 'What does it really mean?'

'Un-un-unlucky chest . . .' quavered timid Thomas beside him. 'It b-brought m-me bad luck. Didn't it?'

'Oh, stop nagging!' cried podgy Plum. 'You're a bit of bad luck yourself, wherever you manage to crawl! Marinka will get on fine. You'll see.'

They waited one hour.

They waited two hours.

hollander

They waited three hours.

The sun crept further and further across the blue sky. The mountains and the palm trees and the white palaces of the Misty East became mistier and mistier in the late afternoon light. There was not a movement to be seen, not a sound to be heard, even the gulls were not crying.

But just as timid Thomas was beginning to snivel, the little Captain said: 'There it comes.'

And sure enough, there was the chest, bobbing out of the harbour on the ebb tide, no bigger than a pin prick. Slowly, very slowly . . .

'It's lying very high,' said podgy Plum.

'Marinka is light,' said the little Captain.

'The luck's gone out of it,' wailed Thomas.

He was right. When at last, at last, they were able to land the chest and open the lid, there seemed to be nothing inside it. No Marinka, no luck.

But there was something inside it: on the bottom lay a sheet of paper and on the paper someone had written in trembling letters (the little Captain read it out): 'Sail into the harbour at midnight. The great lord of Fear and Terror has been . . .'

The last word had been turned into an unreadable splodge by the sea-water.

Fear and Terror?

Three old men sat fishing on the outermost point of the quay. They were doing their best, but the fish did not want to bite.

'Look,' said one. 'I'm making my float turn and turn, but those mackerel down there aren't hungry.'

'Look,' said the second, 'I'm making my float dance and dance, but there is a lemon sole down there, fast asleep.'

'Look,' said the third, 'a chest.'

The three old men forgot their floats and they all watched the chest come floating in on the tide and being bumped against the quay by the waves.

'Perhaps there's a monkey inside,' said one.

'Or dried prunes,' said the second.

But the third man lifted the lid and Marinka stepped out of the chest.

'Didn't think of that, did you?' she said. 'Didn't expect to find me in there!'

'No,' said the fishermen, 'we hadn't thought of that. What a pretty little girl. Or are you a mermaid?'

'I'm not, actually,' said Marinka. 'And I must go to the palace. Can you show me the way?'

'Of course,' said the first little man.

'It's over there,' said the second little man.

But the third little man said: 'They won't let you in.'

'Oho,' said Marinka. 'I've got a message for the great lord of Fear and Terror.'

'The great lord of Fear and Terror?'

'Aha, ehee, oho!' they began to laugh like mad. 'You really are a mermaid, aren't you? You don't know anything about the affairs of men.'

'I am Marinka,' said Marinka.

'Yes, yes! Off to the palace, quickly,' said the three old men, turning back to their three floats. All three had a bite.

Marinka walked to the palace.

It was big and white, being made of marble, and it stood on

eighty-seven pillars. The streets leading to it were crowded, but all the people looked miserable or cross. Their clothes were tattered and there was only one bun on the shelf at the baker's shop.

'It's not very jolly here,' thought Marinka, tugging at the copper bell of the palace.

But the door did not open. Through a shutter, a voice called, 'Not at home! And there's no more money!'

The shutter closed.

'Never say die,' thought Marinka, tugging at the copper bell again, twice, very loudly.

'NOT AT HOME!' the voice shouted through the closed shutter, but Marinka stood on her toes and shouted back: 'I've got some money for you!'

There was immediate silence. Then the shutter opened. 'Wha-whadidyousay?'

'Listen,' said Marinka, 'I've come to bring you seven chests full of treasure for the —'

The palace door flew open and Marinka was drawn inside by a man, large as life, in an apron, large as life, covered with spots and tears.

'Is this a poor country?' asked Marinka.

'Poor, poor, poor,' replied the palace lackey. 'But the cannon are polished.'

'I saw that,' said Marinka. 'But if you start shooting with them you'll get no chests full of treasure.'

The lackey's eyes began to sparkle. 'Where are they?' he asked.

'Shan't tell you that yet,' said Marinka. 'First take me to the great lord of Fear and Terror. He lives here, doesn't he?'

A wave ran down the apron. The man seemed to go limp and leaned against the marble wall for support.

hollander

'Fear and Terror,' he whispered. 'No no . . . yes . . . yes . . . come with me, my girl.'

Before Marinka knew what was happening he was pulling her by one arm, further into the palace. Up marble steps with golden banisters, through empty rooms with mirror floors, along passages of shimmering crystal. At last they came to a door with three thick bolts and three thick curtains and Marinka vanished behind that. Behind the thick curtains, brave Marinka vanished without trace. No more to be seen, no more to be heard – except a chattering of teeth. That was all.

An hour later the three fishermen on the quayside heard running footsteps coming closer. It was the lackey in his apron. But instead of Marinka, he had brought a letter with him.

'The chest!' he cried.

The three fishermen pointed to the chest.

The lackey put the letter inside and pushed the chest off on the ebb tide which carried it out to sea where the *Neversink* lay at anchor.

And when the little Captain had landed the chest and read the letter through three times and read it out to podgy Plum and timid Thomas three times, he said: 'I don't understand. Why didn't Marinka come herself? And what's the matter with the great lord of Fear and Terror?'

'We'll soon see,' said podgy Plum. 'We have to sail in at midnight.'

The setting sun made the copper cannons in the harbour shine with a reddish glow and timid Thomas began to moan softly . . .

The Copper Cannon

'Anchor aweigh!' cried the little Captain.

It was pitch-black night. The half moon had just gone down and all you could see of the stars was the Great Bear and in the harbour there were only three lights.

'I have to steer straight for them,' said the little Captain. 'Then I'll be safe in harbour.'

Podgy Plum blew up the fire under the boiler and the ruddy light of the flames shone on timid Thomas.

Timid Thomas was standing on the foredeck in order to be able to shout whoa! if he saw a rock sticking out of the waves. But his teeth were chattering so hard that he would only have been able to shout k-k-kock, instead of rock.

'Are you as cold as all that, Thomas?' asked podgy Plum between two puffs.

'K-k-k . . .' timid Thomas replied.

'Oh,' said podgy Plum, 'do you mean the c-c-copper c-c-cannon? Well, if they start firing, you'll soon get warm.'

Timid Thomas would have liked to give a shrill scream, but he did not dare do even that. And the *Neversink* sailed calmly into harbour at half power, while the little Captain stood at the helm, feet apart, his eyes on the three little lights.

They were the lights on the quay, and they were slowly coming nearer. Was there anyone watching, or did it only look like it? There was not a movement to be seen, not a sound to be heard. Except for the soft dunk-dunk-dunk of the ship's engine and now and then the wailing whistle of the six-bucket funnel.

And then it happened.

A tremendous explosion, all round the harbour. Boom, thunder and crash of fire, hissing and whistling in the air, and a blinding light.

Timid Thomas's shrill scream burst out now at full strength, but it was quickly smothered because Thomas and his scream jumped into the hold and slammed the hatch shut behind them.

Poor little Thomas! He could not see the splendid fireworks going off over the harbour. Red and green and blue and yellow rockets rushed upwards and burst in a thousand flowers of light. Screamers, crackers, Roman candles, golden rain, Catherine wheels, Chinese parasols and Japanese flashes put the whole town, harbour, houses and all in a dazzling glow of light.

It was the copper cannons.

But instead of aiming cannon-balls at the *Neversink*, they were shooting fireworks into the air as if shouting 'Hurrah!' to the *Neversink*. And there, suddenly, came a real hurrah from the waterside.

'Oooh!' cried podgy Plum. 'Look at all the people! The quay is covered with them. The jetty is wobbling!'

It was a glorious welcome for the *Neversink* at the midnight hour, with many a pom-pom-pom and choruses of ladies, with flags and trumpets and with a torch dance by the loaders and unloaders.

'They must be pleased with the treasure,' said podgy Plum.

'Yes,' said the little Captain.

He brought his boat in alongside the jetty and podgy Plum tied up by the light of the torches.

'Thomas!' he shouted, banging on the hatch. 'Come out now, timid Thomas!'

Timid Thomas's face was paler than the moon. 'A-aren't we dead yet, then?' he asked.

'Of course not,' said podgy Plum, and they stepped ashore, where a group of Misty Eastern reed-pipes, fiddles and mouth-organs were playing a song of welcome.

Timid Thomas was speechless. 'Wh-where is Marinka now?' he asked tearfully.

Marinka was nowhere to be seen, but a man, large as life, in an apron, large as life, came over to them and bowed to the ground.

'Are you the great lord of Fear and Terror?' asked the little Captain.

The man staggered back. 'N-n-ssst!' he uttered. 'I will conduct you.'

He snapped his fingers and twelve soldiers marched up. They were carrying twelve spears and twelve torches. Six of them went

to stand in front of the *Neversink*, grim-faced, to guard the treasures in the hold, for there were many folk about. The other six took the little Captain, podgy Plum and timid Thomas along with them to the white palace on its eighty-seven pillars.

There was a great crowd to be pushed through. The Misty Easterners looked on, in their ragged clothes, their faces questioning in the red light of the torches.

The door to the palace stood open. They walked along marble corridors, through halls with mirror floors, along crystal passages, through the door with the three bolts, and there the three thick curtains were slowly drawn apart.

A vast room lay before them, dimly lighted by a pair of flickering tallow lamps. Here and there stood an old chair.

'I think it's horrid here,' quavered timid Thomas.

He was ready to run away, but someone came towards them out of the half-darkness.

'Hello, hello,' cried a voice. 'Are you here at last?'

It was Marinka.

'Marinka!' Thomas fell sobbing on her neck, but Marinka pushed him away. 'That's not etiquette at court,' she said sharply. 'Come on, little Captain, I will present you.' Marinka pointed to a dais and there, on a battered, worm-eaten wooden throne sat a poor little man with chattering teeth.

The little Captain removed his cap. 'The great lord?' he asked doubtfully, '. . . of Fear and Terror?'

Before the little man on the throne could answer Marinka burst out: 'What? Better and better!' she cried. 'Haven't you even read my letter? I wrote it down: the great lord of Fear and Terror has been dead for ages.'

The First Chest

If only they had known! Then they would not have been so frightened of the Misty East.

Marinka had to laugh. She had not been a prisoner at all: she had been a guardian angel. And now she knew everything.

'Look,' she said, pointing to the battered, worm-eaten, wooden throne on which the poor little man sat with chattering teeth. 'This is the son of the great lord of Fear and Terror.'

'Oh,' said the little Captain.

'He has succeeded his father as lord of the Misty East,' said Marinka. 'But he's different from his father. His name is different, too. He is called the poor lord of Quake and Quiver.'

'You can see that,' said podgy Plum.

'He's even more timid,' said Marinka, 'than timid Thomas.'

'Aha,' said Thomas, sticking his timid chest out quite bravely.

The poor lord of Quake and Quiver raised his head and looked at the four children from the sea. 'The treasure!' he burst out. 'Where are the chests full of treasure?'

But Marinka patted him kindly on his crooked shoulder and said: 'Calm down now, they're coming. First let me tell the whole story.'

And Marinka told them everything she had heard. How the land of the Misty East had fallen into poverty after the death of the great lord of Fear and Terror. How the people grew angrier and angrier. How the poor lord of Quake and Quiver became poorer and quakier and more quivery. And how happy they were now about the seven chests full of treasure.

'Please, please, go and fetch them now!' cried the poor lord pleadingly from his battered throne. 'Then I shall dare to rule again.'

hollander

'All right,' said the little Captain. 'But remember, no more jokes with those copper cannon.'

'Jokes?' cried the poor lord. 'Didn't you think the fireworks were beautiful?'

'Oh yes,' said the little Captain. 'No more firing on ships, I mean. No more cannonballs.'

The poor lord of Quake and Quiver burst out sobbing. 'We weren't doing that any more anyway,' he wept, 'but no ships ever came.'

'And the fireworks were my idea,' said Marinka. 'Good, eh?'

'Not enough whistling rockets,' said podgy Plum. 'Otherwise it was fine.'

'The treasure!' moaned the poor lord. 'Get it now!'

The soldiers went back with them. It was early morning and in the Misty East the sun rises early.

They had not slept all night and timid Thomas was rubbing his eyes. 'Does he get the lucky chest as well?' he asked the little Captain. 'With nothing inside?'

'Of course,' said the little Captain. 'All seven.'

But very soon they were to find out that things were quite different . . .

For on the jetty stood the faithful palace lackey in his ragged apron and when the soldiers were about to unload he said:

'One chest.'

'What did you say?' asked the little Captain.

'Only one chest for the poor lord of Quake and Quiver.'

The little Captain scratched his head under his cap. 'Why?' he asked.

The lackey drew the children after him into the cabin. 'Listen,' he whispered. 'I know all about the treasure. The magician who sent it off long ago put a letter with it, didn't he?'

'Yes,' said the little Captain.

'The treasure was meant for the great lord of Fear and Terror,' said the lackey, 'or . . . after his death for his children . . .'

'Well?' asked podgy Plum.

The lackey straightened. 'The treasure is packed in seven chests,' he said. 'Because the great lord of Fear and Terror had seven children.'

'Seven?' cried Marinka.

'Seven,' repeated the lackey. 'Six sons and one daughter he had. One chest for each. That's how they have to be split up.'

'Ah,' said the little Captain. 'I understand.'

'The letter,' whispered the lackey. 'Show me the letter.'

The little Captain pulled out the old, yellowed and crumpled piece of paper and gave it to the lackey, who began to mumble aloud:

'. . . filled with treasure: crystal bunnies,
copper, silver, rubies red,
diamonds, bigger than your head.
The sixth oak chest is filled with gold,
but luck is what the seventh holds . . .'

'Ha,' said the lackey, 'the eldest son has the first choice. The poor lord of Quake and Quiver chooses the chest full of diamonds!'

The little Captain shrugged his shoulders. 'All right by me,' he said. 'And the other chests? Where are the other sons? And the daughter?'

There was a silence. Then, with a wide sweep of the long sleeves of his overall, the lackey pointed round about him.

'Flown away,' he said miserably. 'Flown from the parental nest! They've scattered to the four winds. Three sons to the Deep South, two sons to the Wild West and the daughter, the youngest, to the Far North.'

Again there was silence. Then Marinka said: 'Well well, it's going to be a long way round.'

'Fine!' cried podgy Plum. 'Then we still don't have to go to school.'

'Boo-hoo!' wept timid Thomas. 'I wouldn't dare to go so far from home!'

The little Captain said nothing, the little Captain stood thinking.

He was thinking of Scurvyboots, the pirate, who had to go on sailing the world on his ship with his hands stuck fast to the helm until the seven chests of treasure had been given back. To the seven children of the great lord of Fear and Terror . . .

When the *Neversink* sailed silently out of harbour an hour later a single chest was standing on the quay. A chest for the poor lord of Quake and Quiver in the Misty East. The other six chests were still on board.

The Ship of the Desert

The south is a very long way off. You have to sail and sail, across a thousand waves and then a thousand more, and the sun rises higher and higher, the shadows grow shorter, until in the end the sun is standing right above your head. Then all the shadows have gone and it is as hot as a baking-oven.

The Deep South lies even further away than that. You have to tip your head right back in order to see the sun, for the sun stands in the north.

The *Neversink* was on her way towards the Deep South, for somewhere there three of the sons of the great lord of Fear and Terror must live. The *Neversink* had six cases of treasure on board and three of them were intended for those sons.

'We must get them there,' said the little Captain, 'because the pirate Scurvyboots has to be set free.'

'Oh, really!' said Marinka. 'What does the fellow matter to us?'

'I see,' said the little Captain, 'so you would just let him bob around on his sailing ship for ever? With his hands stuck fast to the helm?'

Marinka gazed at her feet.

'You know quite well,' the little Captain continued, 'that this is the only way to set Scurvyboots free. By delivering the chests of treasure. To the family of Fear and Terror.'

Marinka bowed her head.

'If I have to sail round the world three times,' said the little Captain, 'it is my duty as a sailor.'

'Hey,' said Marinka, 'I've lost my shadow.'

'Yes,' cried podgy Plum, 'I've lost mine too. I expect timid Thomas has scrubbed them off.'

Timid Thomas hung over the railing with a bucket on a rope, trying to scoop up water. He had to keep the *Neversink's* deck wet against the heat of the sun.

'Shadow gone?' said the little Captain. 'Then we're right on the equator.'

'The equator?' asked timid Thomas. 'Is that something bad?' He almost dropped his bucket.

'It's a blue line,' said Marinka. 'And it divides the world into two halves.'

But however hard Thomas stared into the water he could see no line and the *Neversink* sailed on and on. The sun was left behind in the north, the shadows came back and after seventeen days podgy Plum saw a brown streak in the distance.

'Land!' he cried.

This must be the Deep South, thought the little Captain. He steered straight for it and the brown streak became wavy.

'Lots of little hills!' cried Marinka.

'They're moving!' cried podgy Plum.

The little Captain turned off the engine and steered towards the strange land.

'They're not little hills,' he said. 'They're camels. I think the desert begins there.'

And sure enough, when at last the *Neversink* lay bobbing on the last waves of the sea, the children saw an endless expanse of sand before them. Yellow, dazzling sand, as far as the eye could see.

'Timid Thomas?' cried Marinka. 'Have you got your wooden spoon? And the cutters? You could bake some nice biscuits.'

But timid Thomas didn't dare, because of the camels.

There were ten or so of the humped creatures walking about, rather dreamily, but when they saw the *Neversink* they came inquisitively down to look.

'Do they bite?' asked podgy Plum.

The little Captain shook his head. He jumped ashore and thrust the boat's anchor firmly into the sand.

'Come along!' he cried.

Marinka stroked the camels' noses, podgy Plum patted them on their crooked necks, timid Thomas was still shivering on deck and the little Captain was thinking.

'The ship of the desert,' thought the little Captain. 'We shall have to go still deeper south in order to find the three sons. We might as well change over here from one ship to another.'

That was a good idea. For camels are tremendously strong creatures which can walk through the hot desert for days and days and carry heavy loads as well.

'Listen,' said the little Captain, 'we'll have to go on overland.'

They nodded.

'And we'll have to take the treasure chests with us,' said the little Captain. 'We'll go by camel.'

'No,' shrieked timid Thomas from the *Neversink*. 'Help! I want to go home!'

But whether timid Thomas shrieked or not, he had to help. All six chests were dragged out of the hold one by one and carried ashore. Each camel was given two to carry, one on each side of his body, with a rope tied over his back.

'We only have to deliver three chests,' said podgy Plum.

'But we can hardly leave the rest in the hold. What if pirates were to come while we were gone?'

'P-pirates?' quavered Thomas. And he decided that it would be better to stay with the others after all and travel with them by camel.

So the procession set off. Four camels, each with a child on its front hump, and three camels with two chests on each side. The last camel walked crooked, because it had the lucky chest tied on one side and that was always empty . . .

Would they find anyone in the endless, endless desert sand?

Mirage

'It keeps rolling!' cried timid Thomas. He had been saying the same thing for hours, for they had already been travelling for hours, on their camels, across the endless desert. The dry, hot, flat, empty, silent desert sand.

'I'm going to be seasick!' cried timid Thomas.

'Camel-sick, you mean,' said Marinka. 'Eat a cream cake. It helps.'

'Oolf!' went timid Thomas, looking as yellow as the sand.

On they went, deeper and deeper south. Podgy Plum was puffing with the heat. 'Little Captain,' he asked, 'where do we come out?'

But the little Captain did not answer. He steered his camel straight ahead, the reins taut in his hand, his eyes on the horizon.

On they went, hour after hour after hour.

'I'm stifling with heat,' cried podgy Plum.

'I'm dying of thirst,' sighed Marinka.

'I want to be sick,' moaned timid Thomas.

Then the little Captain called a halt, they dismounted and rested on the burning sand to have something to eat and drink.

'Isn't the sand beautiful,' said Marinka. 'You can write your name all over it — ouch!' She was trying it out with her finger, but it was too hot. A stick worked better. '*Marinka was here*,' she wrote in the sand. 'You never know,' she said, 'if they might have to come and rescue us.'

'Rescue?' asked timid Thomas in a timid voice. 'Th-then are we los . . .'

Timid Thomas got no further. His voice stuck in his throat. He stared into the distance with bulging eyes.

'What's the matter, Thomas?' asked podgy Plum.

But timid Thomas did not answer. He stood up like a pale ghost, put his hands out in front of him and began to walk. Towards nothing. Towards the far horizon which was nothing but a misty line.

'Thomas?' called Marinka.

'Here!' called podgy Plum.

But the little Captain said: 'He's seeing a mirage.'

It was true. Timid Thomas could see something the others could not see. He could see a garden, the most beautiful garden from his most beautiful dream, with waving trees and pretty flowers and pleasant arbours. And with a fountain which spurted cool, fresh, clear water.

It was not really there, the whole garden was not there, but people who journey across the desert and are thirsty from having the hot sun on their heads suddenly see things like that in front of them — in their imagination.

'A mirage,' cried the little Captain (because that is its name). 'Catch him!'

'But I can't see anything,' said podgy Plum.

'I mean catch Thomas,' shouted the little Captain. 'Quick!'

The three of them dragged timid Thomas back, but the poor little chap began to howl.

'I'm so thirsty! I want to go to the garden. Let me go!'

He tugged, he hit out, he scratched, he bit. Timid Thomas had turned into Thomas the Terror. They could not get him under control, he kept on running away, and in the end the little Captain said: 'Well, put him in the empty chest.'

It was the only hope.

The three camels with the treasure chests were still lying patiently in the sand. The empty chest, the lucky chest, was opened and timid Thomas was put inside.

Poor Thomas. It was even hotter there than outside, but however much he shrieked and howled, the lid stayed shut — with a crack for air, of course.

And on they went. Lucky for Thomas, who would otherwise have vanished for ever into the desert; lucky for the camel, which could walk straight now because the chest on one side was just as heavy as the chest on the other side.

The sun began to sink and then it was the little Captain who gave a shout.

'An oasis!' cried the little Captain.

hollander

'What?' asked podgy Plum. 'Another dream garden?'

'No,' said the little Captain. 'This is a real one.'

'Do you know for sure?' asked Marinka. 'Aren't you very thirsty?'

'Oh yes,' said the little Captain, 'I'm very thirsty, but the palm trees there are real.'

The little Captain was right. A quarter of an hour later they were standing in the shadow of the leaves and drinking water from the well. Cool, clear water.

'Then is this the garden timid Thomas saw?' asked Marinka. She opened the lid of the chest. 'Thomas, we're there!'

But timid Thomas had fallen asleep. He was snoring like an ox.

'Leave him alone,' said the little Captain. 'He'll wake up on his own soon and then he'll be quite all right again.'

Then night fell, the pitch-black night of the desert, where there is no other light than that of a thousand sparkling stars above your head. Where there is no shadow, for everything is black.

And yet . . . shadows were moving about. Creeping shadows, slowly approaching the oasis.

Timid Thomas's Trail

The desert on the way to the Deep South is not entirely uninhabited. Here and there there are hills with caverns and passages in them and in the caves live robbers. Robbers lying in wait for long-distance travellers, on camels, carrying spoils.

That night two rode out on fast, silent horses, for in the distance they had seen a caravan, a caravan of seven camels.

'It looks as if there are children on the humps,' said one.

'Children? That's nothing!' said the other. 'I can see baggage. I can see chests. Heavy chests. Spoils!'

In the dark night they rode towards the oasis, stealthily — the robbers Borrow and Morrow.

'What shall we do?' asked Morrow. 'Get the whole place in an uproar with enough noise for ten?'

'We'll be like ghosts,' said Borrow. 'We won't make any noise, we'll only take the camels.'

The night breeze rustled softly in the trees as the two shadows crept forward and untied the camels' ropes with swift fingers. The good, patient, obedient creatures got to their feet and followed the two dark figures over the rippling sand.

Without a sound the procession left the oasis.

The three children who were sleeping peacefully beside the well, dreaming of glorious flower gardens with fountains in them, did not even move.

'Spoils!' hissed Morrow. 'We've got the spoils.' He wanted to look inside the chest straight away but Borrow gave him a shove. 'Get your greedy fingers off! Time enough to count it all when we're home again.'

They mounted their horses and drove the camels away into the dim desert.

What the robbers Borrow and Morrow had not noticed was that the lid of one of the chests was slightly open. And that the two timid eyes of a timid little boy were staring out. A boy too timid to shout for help. How could the robbers have known that timid Thomas had been sleeping inside one of the treasure chests?

hollander

When the camel moved off, timid Thomas woke up with a shock. Timid Thomas yawned, stared through the crack, wanted to yell, but saw two black ghosts which made both yawn and yell stick in his gullet. He wanted to jump out of the chest but dared not, clutched at a branch but it was a dead one, hanging loose on the tree.

The whole chest quivered with Thomas's terror. 'Help!' he wanted to shout. 'Help, help, I'm being stolen and kidnapped.' But not a sound came from his throat. Then he stuck the branch out to wave, but who could see it in the dark night? Not even the robbers.

'Help, help!' But timid Thomas was not shouting, he was writing. He was writing as Marinka had done, in the sand, with his branch.

The camels plodded on under the thousand, thousand pinprick lights of the stars above the endless desert. Camels with nothing, and camels with chests, and the last camel leaving a strange track behind it. It looked like a doodle on a scribbling-pad.

When the distant sun rose from the yellow sand like a red ball of fire, podgy Plum woke up. He rubbed his eyes, sniffed, scratched his head and looked about him. 'Hallo,' thought podgy Plum, 'it looks just as if something that should be there isn't there. But what?' He looked across at the little Captain, sleeping with his cap over his eyes. He looked at Marinka, rolled up on the sand like a cat. He looked at —

Ah! Suddenly podgy Plum knew: timid Thomas wasn't there.

'Thomas!' he shouted. 'Timid Thomas! Where are you?'

Timid Thomas might be leaning against a tree somewhere, thought Plum, but more and more time passed and he failed to appear.

'Hallo!' cried Marinka suddenly, yawning. 'Where are the camels?'

'The *camels*!' Podgy Plum shouted so loudly that the little Captain was also awakened. 'The camels have gone! And timid Thomas too!'

The little Captain got to his feet and looked at the tracks in the sand. 'They're a few hours old,' he said.

'The traitor!' cried podgy Plum. 'He's made off in the middle of the night with all the treasure.'

'Timid Thomas wouldn't dare do anything like that,' said Marinka.

The little Captain was following the tracks.

'The creatures wouldn't go off by themselves, would they?' said podgy Plum. 'We had tied them up securely, too. Someone untied the knots. Who could it have been but Thomas?'

'Well,' said Marinka, 'perhaps he's gone back to the *Neversink* then.'

'No!' cried podgy Plum. 'I know! He's gone to his garden, of course! To his dream garden.'

The little Captain was still following the camel tracks. 'That's odd,' he muttered suddenly. 'Look here.'

There were funny scratches in the sand, a sort of quavering line.

'Like doodling,' said podgy Plum.

But Marinka gave a little shriek. 'There's something there,' she cried. 'Writing! Have a look: you can read it!'

Now the little Captain and podgy Plum could see it too. A quavering line of letters, all joined together, reaching to the horizon: helphelphelphelp . . .

'Timid Thomas,' said the little Captain. 'Timid Thomas and the camels have been kidnapped. By robbers . . .'

What the Robbers Forgot

The robbers Borrow and Morrow had a brother. His name was Allmysorrow and he played on his accordion all day long. Allmysorrow was not at all a good robber; he did not even have a horse. He had a donkey, on which he rode backwards, so that he could hold on to its tail.

Allmysorrow never wanted to go out robbing with his brothers. 'You and your donkey!' said Borrow and Morrow. But that didn't worry Allmysorrow. He was not all that keen on getting rich. He preferred to stay at home in the cave where they lived and cook their dinners and play on his accordion and sing the most delightful songs:

'The robber's little laddie
had a shotgun for his play.
He shot his Mum, he shot his Daddie
and he grew deafer every day.'

When Borrow and Morrow returned home from their night's outing with the camels Allmysorrow had to help unload the chests and carry them into the cave.

'Heavy, aren't they!' he cried. 'They must be full of sand.'

'Sand, fiddlesticks,' said Borrow.

'Let's have a look,' said Morrow.

They had opened the first chest and were staring, wide-eyed, at the contents.

'Oh, just gold,' said Allmysorrow. 'Where's the music in that?'

They opened the second chest.

'Silver!' cried Borrow and Morrow, their eyes greedy.

'I'd have you know,' said Allmysorrow, 'that I've no intention of polishing all that lot.'

The third chest was full of copper. Allmysorrow did not even bother to look.

The fourth chest glittered with red rubies, but Allmysorrow picked up his accordion. 'What a lot of rubbish,' he said, and began to play a little air.

But when Borrow and Morrow opened the fifth chest and they themselves cried 'Oh, what rubbish!' Allmysorrow got up curiously to have a look.

'Oh,' he cried, 'that's beautiful!'

The chest was full of crystal rabbits.

'You can have that one, then,' said Borrow and Morrow. 'You can have a nice game with it.'

Crystal sings if you tap it gently. Allmysorrow placed the rabbits in a ring and made music on them with his fingers. Pling-plang-plong, they went. Allmysorrow was enchanted.

Then Borrow and Morrow opened the last chest.

That was full of little boy.

'What's this?' cried Morrow.

'What indeed!' cried Borrow. 'A little slave. We can sell him off well.'

Poor Thomas. He was still unable to utter a word. He could

not even shout for help; it would not have helped him anyway.

Borrow picked him up out of the chest and Morrow felt his arms.

'Useless little scrag-end,' he said. 'No fat, no muscle. Good for nothing.'

'N-no!' timid Thomas managed to stammer out at last. 'I shall never do it again.'

'Never do what again?' asked Borrow.

'R-run away,' hiccupped timid Thomas.

'Run away? Did you run away?'

'I-I-I saw a garden,' said timid Thomas. 'A very beautiful garden, and then —'

'What?' It was Allmysorrow who shouted. He left his singing rabbits and came over to Thomas. 'A garden with trees and flowers and arbours and a fountain?' he asked.

Timid Thomas nodded palely.

'There you are, you see!' Allmysorrow cried to his brothers. 'You never believed me, did you? When I said I saw the garden! Now what do you say?'

Borrow and Morrow looked at each other. Robbers don't believe in fairy tales, but now that two people had spoken of the mysterious garden in the desert they began to have doubts.

'Who knows,' muttered Borrow.

'We've got enough money now,' whispered Morrow.

'And you wouldn't have to go on being robbers any more,' said Allmysorrow. 'We could go and live there in peace.'

Borrow and Morrow looked at timid Thomas. 'He can rake leaves,' they said.

'No!' yelled timid Thomas. 'I want to go back. Back to the little Captain.'

But the little Captain was far away. He was standing in the middle of the desert with Marinka and podgy Plum, shaking his head gloomily.

'We'll never catch up,' said the little Captain. 'We can follow this helphelphelp trail, but without our camels we'll never overtake the robbers.'

He had realized that this was robbers' work.

All they could do was to return to the oasis. The sun was already beginning to burn.

'Thomas!' sobbed Marinka. 'Treasure!'

'Well,' said podgy Plum. 'I didn't think timid Thomas was all that much of a treasure, you know.'

'No!' howled Marinka. 'I mean we've lost timid Thomas and the treasure.'

'Oh,' said podgy Plum. 'Well, what now? We can't even get back to the *Neversink*.'

Marinka had not thought of that.

The little Captain had.

The little Captain was looking pretty gloomy. They would have to stay at the oasis until another caravan passed by. That might take weeks or months and what would become of timid Thomas? Now that the treasure chests had been stolen, they would not be able to release Scurvyboots the pirate from his ghost ship, either. The little Captain had never been so full of gloomy thoughts.

But at that very moment he heard Marinka shouting. Marinka had run ahead and disappeared among the trees of the oasis. 'Left!' she was shouting. 'Left, left!'

The little Captain and podgy Plum ran towards her. Marinka was standing at the far end of the oasis, and beside her stood —

'Oh!' said podgy Plum, 'she was saying "there's one left!"'

For beside Marinka stood the two-humped animal on which timid Thomas had been riding before he had been packed into the chest.

The robbers had forgotten one camel . . .

A Mirror in the Sky

Quicker than lightning, the three children jumped on the camel's back. The little Captain sat on the front hump, Marinka between the two humps and podgy Plum on the back hump.

'Full steam ahead!' cried the little Captain, but that didn't help. The camel was not the *Neversink*.

Podgy Plum blew out his cheeks, but of course the camel had no furnace to be stoked, either.

'Gee up!' cried Marinka. That was animal talk. The camel understood that. It rose to its feet and began to walk, but it walked very slowly and sleepily.

'*Hup hup hup*!' cried Marinka. 'Faster.' She drummed the animal's sides with her heels. That helped. The camel began to trot, to canter, to gallop. Marinka's heels tickled.

The little Captain steered with his legs clamped fast on the front hump and his eyes on timid Thomas's trail — the helphelphelp trail which led in a quavering line across the sand to the horizon.

'Faster, faster! *Hup hup hup*!' Marinka went on encouraging the camel and the good beast galloped on, hour after hour.

'I can see something!' cried podgy Plum suddenly.

'Hills!' cried the little Captain.

'And rocks!' cried podgy Plum. 'Rocks with caves in them.'

The trail led straight to them.

'Careful, now,' said Marinka. 'The robbers are there.'

But the little Captain rode on at full gallop. The little Captain was not afraid, not even of forty thieves.

'*Hup*!' he himself now shouted to the camel, steering straight for the biggest and darkest cave, the cave of Borrow, Morrow and Allmysorrow.

'Hey there!' shouted the little Captain. 'I'll get you, you nasty robbers!'

'Robbers!' came the answer, but it was only an echo. The camel stopped just at the entrance. The little Captain and podgy Plum jumped down. Marinka stayed where she was — she didn't like it.

'*Yoohoo*!' called podgy Plum.

'*Hoohoohoo*!' echoed the cave.

Marinka liked it even less. 'They're waiting to ambush you,' she whispered shakily.

But the little Captain walked inside. All he found in the half darkness was a blackened cauldron and a single crystal rabbit which Allmysorrow had left behind.

The robbers had gone, with timid Thomas, the camels and the treasure chests.

What now? There were so many tracks by the cave that it was impossible to see which way the robbers had gone. And timid Thomas had not written any more.

Suddenly Marinka began to sob. 'We'll never find them again,' she wept. 'Never again.'

Podgy Plum gave the cauldron a hefty kick. The thing rolled several yards across the sand and bumped into the crystal rabbit. *Pling*! went the crystal rabbit.

'*Pling*!' said podgy Plum furiously. He was going to kick the rabbit too, but Marinka picked it up. 'Leave it!' she cried. 'I want to keep it.'

The little Captain was standing outside in the sand, legs planted firmly apart, staring grave-eyed towards the horizon. 'Bless my soul,' said the little Captain, narrowing his eyes and looking again. There, just above the horizon, he saw a sparkling dream garden hanging in the air, just as timid Thomas had done.

The little Captain pinched himself. 'I'm not dreaming,' he muttered, 'and I'm not thirsty. And yet I can see a mirage. So it must be real. A real garden, over the horizon.'

The little Captain was right. The garden which timid Thomas had seen in his imagination really did exist. It was an old, deserted garden, with a tumbledown palace where an exiled

hollander

sheik had once lived. And sometimes, in the heat of the day, you could see the ruins and the trees and the flowers up in the air, because hot air sometimes acts as a mirror, just like water.

'Aha,' thought the little Captain, 'I think the robbers have gone there.'

He called Marinka and podgy Plum and the three of them mounted the camel again, the three of them said 'Gee up!' all together and made straight for the place where they had seen the reflection in the sky.

The little Captain had been right again. The robbers were on their way to the secret garden. But Allmysorrow did not know the place exactly, because he always rode back to front on his donkey, and timid Thomas did not know the place at all. The camels with their heavy treasure chests trailed sluggishly through the sand and Borrow and Morrow grew more and more impatient. 'Where is it, then?' they kept crying. 'Where is it then?' And timid Thomas pointed with a shaking finger: 'There!' But Allmysorrow would cry: 'No, no, there!' And so the robber caravan and the treasures rode across the desert in swoops and semi-circles.

But the camel carrying the little Captain, Marinka and podgy Plum rode in a straight line, at the gallop.

And when at last, at last, at last, the first robber, Borrow, saw something sparkling in the distance which looked like a garden, a real garden with walls and a gateway, and when, after endless jolting, they reached the beautiful golden gate, there was a camel standing there with three children on its back, barring the way.

'Halt!' they heard. 'Give back the stolen treasures! They belong with me. I am the little Captain.'

Three More Chests

There they stood. One camel, carrying the little Captain, Marinka and podgy Plum, facing six camels, two horses and a donkey, with the robbers Borrow, Morrow and Allmysorrow on their backs, as well as the treasure chests and whimpering Thomas.

The golden gate of the garden which was no longer a mirage stood wide open.

'Ha, ha,' laughed Borrow. 'Are you going to stop us?'

'Choose!' laughed Morrow. 'Shall we throw you in the fountain or in the sand?'

'Look out, look out!' sang Allmysorrow. 'They'll knock you about.'

But the little Captain looked straight into their faces.

'Robbers,' he said, 'give back the treasure. And the camels.'

'Well,' cried Borrow, 'do you mean they're yours?'

'No,' said the little Captain, 'they are not mine. But —'

'Well, then!' laughed Borrow. His teeth flashed.

'Out of the way!' cried Morrow. His knife slashed.

'And as for you,' sang Allmysorrow, 'we'll cut you in two.'

But the little Captain was not afraid. The little Captain went on sitting calmly on the camel's front hump, because the little Captain had not finished speaking. He said: 'The treasures belong to the sons of the great lord of Fear and Terror. That's where we're taking them.'

He might have pronounced a spell. The knife fell from Morrow's hands, Borrow's mouth fell wide open and Allmysorrow fell off his donkey.

'*What?*' cried all three robbers together. And then they shouted something else, their voices hoarse. They shouted: 'It's *Father's?*' There was a tremendous hubbub. Timid Thomas thought they were fighting and buried his face in his hands, but it was not a fight, it was a dance of joy. Borrow and Morrow leaped about on the sand like madmen. Allmysorrow billowed away on his accordion, the horses whinnied, the donkey brayed and the camels stood primly by.

Timid Thomas stopped his ears, but Marinka and podgy Plum sat staring wide-eyed at the strange spectacle.

'Wh-what does it all mean?' asked podgy Plum.

'It means,' said the little Captain, 'that we have found them.'

'Who's *them?*' asked Marinka.

The little Captain pointed to the dancing robbers. 'Those are three of the sons of the great lord of Fear and Terror,' he said. 'Just as I thought. They weren't real robbers at all.'

Then Marinka's mouth opened wide. 'How could you tell?' she asked.

For answer the little Captain pulled an old, crumpled, yellowed piece of paper out of his pocket. It was the letter which had been with the treasure chests. 'Do you remember the last few lines?' he said, and he read them aloud:

'And as for theft, rely on me!
A thieving hand would, through my spell,
be clamped for ever to the wheel.'
'Scurvyboots?' asked podgy Plum.

'Yes, Scurvyboots,' said the little Captain. 'But it applies to other robbers too. Borrow's, Morrow's and Allmysorrow's hands would have stuck to the camels' reins if they had been robbers. But they are the sons of the great lord himself.'

Meanwhile the sons had gone leaping and singing and jumping through the golden gate into the garden.

'Listen,' cried Borrow. 'We're going to build this ruined palace up again, because we have gold in plenty.'

'Listen,' cried Morrow. 'We're going to live here from now on, because we have silver without end.'

'Listen,' cried Allmysorrow. 'The crystal rabbits! They pling and plong so prettily.'

'SILENCE!' ordered the little Captain. He was standing in the middle. 'You have chosen,' he said. 'A chest each; the one filled with gold, the silver, and the crystal rabbits. Take them! The rest goes back with us, because now we shall have to go in search of the other two sons who went to the Wild West. And the only daughter, who lives in the Far North.'

hollander

'NO!' cried timid Thomas. 'I want to go home.'

'HELP!' shrieked timid Thomas, because Borrow suddenly picked him up and threw him through the air to Morrow, who threw him to Allmysorrow, who threw him back to Borrow. 'We'll keep you here!' they cried, laughing. 'As a gardener's boy.'

But that was a joke. After a feast under the rustling trees of the secret garden, there in the Deep South, the four children set off again on their camels with the remaining treasure chests towards the coast where the *Neversink* lay at anchor. Three long, hot days they spent on the journey, but they had enough to eat and drink and the little Captain's brave little boat lay bobbing on the blue waves, waiting for them.

The three treasure chests were placed in the hold. Podgy Plum blew up the furnace, Marinka made some more pancake dough, timid Thomas began to swab obediently and the little Captain pulled the steam whistle. It was a goodbye whistle to the seven camels which had carried them so kindly and which could now wander about freely again in the desert where they felt so much at home.

The little Captain set course for the west. The sun went down, the moon came up, and then, just before they were going to bed, all four of them at once saw a great white bird. No, not a bird. Sails. The sails of a sailing ship, the ghost ship of Scurvyboots. The old pirate was at the wheel. 'Maties!' he bellowed. 'Maties! Look!'

The little Captain, podgy Plum, Marinka and timid Thomas saw him waving. Waving one arm wildly in the air, as he flew past like a phantom.

'Look at that,' muttered the little Captain. 'We have handed over half the treasure. One arm has already been released from the spell.'

Westward Ho!

The west lies where the sun sets. You would think that there was an enormously deep pit at that spot for the sun to crawl into, so that the world turns dark. But where exactly is the pit? In a meadow, in a wood, among the mountains? Or in the sea? Of course it couldn't be in the sea. But the west must be somewhere, mustn't it?

The *Neversink* had been sailing for weeks, straight for the west. The little Captain never once turned off course. He held the wheel in his fists without giving it a single twist, and there he stood, feet apart, eyes on the horizon, where the sun sank every day.

But the place was as far away as ever.

Marinka had used up all the flour on pancakes, podgy Plum had put all the coal on the fire and timid Thomas's swab had not a hair left on it. Timid Thomas had no tears left either: he had wept them all out of his eyes with sorrow, because the *Neversink* was still not going home. He was looking forward to going back to school so much!

'We'll be in the west soon, you'll see,' Marinka comforted him. But timid Thomas didn't like the sound of that either, because it meant that they would plunge into the enormous pit, boat and all.

'We shall have to put into harbour somewhere,' said the little Captain, 'to lay in provisions.'

'And to ask the way,' said podgy Plum.

'And to buy fresh tears,' said Marinka, 'because timid Thomas is drying out completely.'

The first harbour they came to was the port of Xuxuxalpetl. A little village on the bay of a forgotten coast, set among cliffs, no more than five houses and a pub. A sailors' pub.

And in the five houses lived five old sea captains who sat playing cards all day in the sailors' pub. They drank black beer with foam on top and all they said was 'Five of hearts' or 'Ace of clubs' and now and again 'Trump!'

'Trump!' one of the old sea captains was just saying, when the little Captain in his big cap came striding in.

'Great heavens above!' all five cried together, and it was the first time for years that they had said anything but 'Five of hearts' or 'Ace of clubs'.

'Good-day all,' said the little Captain, touching his cap politely. 'Could you please tell me where the west actually lies?'

The five old sea captains looked at each other. Then their big mouths opened all together and they began to roar with laughter. 'The west! Ho ho ho! A captain, asking for the west!' And they banged the little Captain on the shoulder so that he almost sank through the floor; it was the best joke they had ever heard.

'Beer!' they cried. 'A mug of beer for the young captain!' And they pushed him into a chair and all five came to sit round him and poured the mug down his throat.

The little Captain was forced to drink. He got a white moustache and a white beard from the foam and the black beer made him feel dizzy and giddy.

'Cheers!' they cried. 'Can you play cards?'

But the little Captain could no longer tell the difference between the five of hearts and the ace of clubs. They danced before his eyes, he slumped against the table, his cap askew over his nose and with a loud yawn he fell asleep, snoring like a real, big, old sea captain.

'Heavens above. . . !'

The five sea captains gazed at him as if their own ships had run aground in the open sea.

'What kind of a captain is that?' asked number one.

'After only one mug!' cried number two.

'Could he have been an exhausted castaway?' asked number three.

'I wonder where he comes from?' murmured number four.

'Let's see if he's got any papers on him,' suggested number five.

They searched through his clothes. Out of the little Captain's trouser pocket came a handkerchief, marked L.C., a pretty pink

hollander

shell and a compass. Out of his back pocket came a rope's end, a rusty nail and a penny piece. Out of his jacket pocket came a bit of wire, two little wheels, a rubber and a map of the blue sea. Out of his breast pocket came a yellowing photograph. 'Could that have been his mother?' asked one of the sea captains. They were quiet for a moment, so that only the snores of the little captain could be heard. Then they felt in his inside pocket.

'Aha! A letter!'

They bumped into each other, put pairs of rusty steel-rimmed spectacles on their noses and began to read aloud: 'To the great lord of Fear and Terror,' and underneath:

Herewith the seven chests! Each one is
filled with treasure: crystal bunnies,
copper, silver, rubies red,
diamonds, bigger than your head.
The sixth oak chest is filled with gold,
but luck is what the seventh holds.
I send them to you, sir, by sea,
and as for theft, rely on me!
A thieving hand would, through my spell,
be clamped for ever to the wheel.'

The five sea captains took off their five rusty pairs of glasses and looked at each other.

'There's something fishy about this,' they muttered. 'This talk of treasures and robbers won't do. They're sure to want to go through the lock gates . . .'

On board the *Neversink*, podgy Plum and Marinka and timid Thomas who were waiting for the little Captain to come back, grew anxious.

The little Captain had been gone a long, long time . . .

Where is the little Captain?

When, after three whole hours, the little Captain had still not returned, Marinka said: 'I'll go and look for him.'

All that time the three of them had been sitting waiting in the cabin of the *Neversink*, where it lay moored in the harbour of Xuxuxalpetl.

'I'll go with you,' said podgy Plum.

Timid Thomas was already beginning to turn pale. 'Must I stay here to l-look after the ship?' he asked. For timid Thomas always had to do that.

'Of course,' said Marinka. 'And if anyone comes, just pull on the steam whistle. Once for a thief, twice for a raider and three times for the little Captain.'

Timid Thomas tried to remember this while Marinka and podgy Plum walked towards the little square of five houses and a pub. Timid Thomas would have liked to creep into the hold, but then he would not be able to reach the steam whistle cord.

'Sea-folk always go to the pub first,' said Marinka firmly, and she stepped bravely into the tap-room, followed by podgy Plum.

'Great heavens above,' cried the five sea captains, 'still more children!'

'We're looking for the little Captain,' said Marinka. 'Has he been here?'

'Been? Ho ho ho!' The sea captains roared with laughter and pointed to the floor behind the bar. There lay the little Captain, still snoring after the black beer.

'Is he ill?' asked Marinka anxiously.

'No, no,' said podgy Plum. 'He's tired. He's been standing at the wheel for eight days on end.'

The five sea captains looked at each other. 'Running away, I suppose?' they said. 'With all those treasures on board?'

'What?' cried Marinka. 'How did you get hold of that?'

The five sea captains showed her the old, crumpled and yellowed piece of paper that they had found in the little Captain's inside pocket. 'It says so here,' they said.

'But hasn't the little Captain told you what it means?' asked Marinka.

'He was asleep,' they said.

Then Marinka and podgy Plum told the whole story: of Scurvyboots the pirate who had stolen the seven chests long ago and, as a punishment, had had to sail the seven seas on his ghost ship ever since. He could be released when the seven chests had been delivered and the little Captain was doing that now, but the seven chests had to be taken to the children of the great lord of Fear and Terror, because the great lord himself had been dead for a long time. They told how they had handed over the first chest, full of huge diamonds, to the eldest son in the Misty East, the next three chests to the three sons who lived in the Deep South, and were now on their way to the Wild West, where two more sons had gone, and —

'The Wild West?' cried the five sea captains. 'Great heavens above! The Wild West is the Boiling Sea. Behind here.'

They pointed with their five thick thumbs through the wall of the tap-room. 'Not a soul can live there.'

Marinka stiffened.

But podgy Plum asked: 'What is the Boiling Sea, then?'

'That, young matey,' said the sea captains, 'is the most dangerous sea there is. So dangerous that it is not shown on any map. When there is a storm there, and there is a storm about three times a day, you get slam, bang and bubble waves which smash your ship to smithereens before you can count up to thirteen and suck it to the bottom.'

'Oh,' said Marinka. 'But the little Captain is not afraid of anything.'

'Well, well,' said the five.

'And our boat, the *Neversink*, can stand up to a few knocks,' said podgy Plum.

'Well, well,' said the five. 'Then we had better tell you that there is only one vessel in existence which can sail the Boiling

hollander

Sea. A ship as big as a town. It comes here just once a year, and that ship is the only one we ever allow through the lock.'

'Through the lock?' asked podgy Plum. 'Is there a lock here?'

'You bet your life, what did you think? That you could just sail into the Boiling Sea? They made a fine watergate for it. And we look after it.'

'Oh,' said Marinka, 'so the *Neversink* . . .' Then she had an idea: 'This once-a-year ship, when will it be coming again?'

'Just been,' said the five sea captains. 'Two days back.'

Podgy Plum and Marinka stared at the ground. What were they to do? How would they ever get into the Boiling Sea, and still worse: would they be able to find the two sons there? After all, if no one could live there . . .

'Little Captain!' cried Marinka, and she ran to the bar to shake him awake.

But the little Captain was not lying behind the bar; he was not in the taproom at all. The little Captain had gone.

'Eh?' said Marinka.

But podgy Plum raised a finger. 'Listen!'

In the distance they heard the *Neversink's* steam whistle. Three shrill notes.

'He's back on board! Come on!'

But when Marinka and podgy Plum rushed up the gang-plank, the only person they met was a pale Thomas.

'Th-thieves,' stammered Thomas, 'I thought I heard thieves. Th-th-three thieves.'

There was no one to be seen, not even the little Captain. Where was the little Captain?

The Boiling Sea

The little Captain had woken up behind the bar while Marinka and podgy Plum were talking to the five sea captains. He had heard all about the Boiling Sea, and about the ship as big as a town and about the lock gate.

'The lock gate!' thought the little Captain and like a mouse he stole out of the back door of the tap room. 'If I can open the lock gate,' thought the little Captain, 'I shall sail through it with the *Neversink*.' For the little Captain must and would get to the Wild West, even if there was a Boiling Sea in which every ship was wrecked. The *Neversink* was not called 'never sink' for nothing.

The lock gate lay at the end of the little sea port and in order to open it you had to turn a wheel. It was heavy work and it squeaked, but the little Captain strained and sweated until the big watergate stood ajar, wide enough to let the *Neversink* through.

Then, at the run, the little Captain returned to the quay where his boat was moored. He had heard the steam whistle blow three times and he realized that the others were on board and growing anxious.

'Here I am,' he cried, jumping on deck. 'Quick, anchor aweigh. Full steam ahead.'

'But little Captain!' cried Marinka. 'Where —'

'Sssh,' said the little Captain, grasping the helm.

'Little Captain,' cried podgy Plum, 'there's nowhere —'

'Sssh,' said the little Captain, steering out of the harbour.

'Little Captain!' screeched timid Thomas. 'We're not going, not going to . . .' For timid Thomas had been hearing all the tales of the Boiling Sea.

But the little Captain nodded. 'We're going,' he said, and he steered straight for the open lock gate.

The five old sea captains were about to start playing cards again when they heard the little boat leaving. They glanced out of the window and waved their arms. 'Goodbye,' they muttered, and then their arms stiffened in the air. 'Great heavens above!' they cried. 'He's sailing for the lock!'

As one man, they rushed out of the door. 'Hey, halt, stop!' they roared to the *Neversink*. 'Close the lock gate,' they told each other.

The *Neversink* sped through the water under full power.

The five sea captains flew puffing along the quay.

The *Neversink* reached the lock first.

As the sea captains began to turn the wheel to close the lock gate, the little boat just slipped through the narrow gap and the foaming water spattered the faces of the sea captains.

'You're mad!' they roared. 'Little madcap, you're as mad as a hatter!'

For answer came the piercing shriek of the steam whistle as the little Captain tugged it and then the piercing screech of timid Thomas, as he saw the Boiling Sea opening up ahead of him.

'Great heavens above,' muttered the five big sea captains, 'that crazy clown is heading straight for disaster,' and they stared in silence at the doughty little boat, until they had to put their five pairs of rusty steel glasses back on their noses, it had grown so small.

The *Neversink* sailed bravely on. The waves were calm — no slam, bang or bubble; the Boiling Sea was still, for the wind was having a day of rest.

Timid Thomas had fled to the hold and was sitting there in the seventh chest, the empty good-luck chest, which seemed to him the safest place.

Marinka and podgy Plum were standing by the wheel, looking pale.

'Little Captain,' Marinka began, 'you do know that every ship is wrecked when there's a storm here?'

'Yes,' said the little Captain.

'Little Captain,' said podgy Plum, 'wouldn't it be better for us to wait for the ship as big as a town and cross the sea on that?'

'No,' said the little Captain.

The colour of the water was dark grey, because the Boiling Sea was thirteen fathoms deep. And the coast was a high wall of

hollander

steep cliffs, for the Boiling Sea was in the shape of an enormous saucepan half full of water.

The little Captain tugged at the steam whistle and the echo travelled to and fro thirteen times, from one rocky shore to another and back again.

'They must have heard that,' he said, 'so they will come out by themselves.'

'Who?'

'The sons, of course. The two sons of the great lord of Fear and Terror. They must be somewhere here.'

Every quarter of an hour the little Captain blew the whistle, but nothing appeared and so they sailed on, hour after hour, until dusk began to fall.

And then — 'Listen!' cried podgy Plum — it seemed as if there was an answer. Another steam whistle, far away in the distance. At the same moment all three of them saw it, faintly, on the horizon: houses, roofs, towers, windmills.

'A town!' shouted Marinka.

'How can that be?' cried podgy Plum.

The little Captain said: 'It's the ship. It's a floating town.'

'Where, where?' asked timid Thomas, who had bounced up out of the hold with relief.

But timid Thomas saw nothing, because it was suddenly dark. Not because the sun had gone down, but because clouds had blown up, pitch-black clouds, ink-black clouds.

Storm clouds . . .

The Storm

The five sea captains had been playing cards in their inn for a long time when the storm burst.

'Eight of clubs,' said one. 'Wind force ten.'

'Ten of clubs,' said another. 'Wind force twelve.'

'Trump!' cried the third. 'It's a hurricane.'

And a hurricane it was. The wind flung itself, howling, on the roofs of Xuxuxalpetl, blew the roof tiles through the air like fluttering leaves and smashed the chimneys on the streets below. 'Jack of diamonds,' said the fourth sea captain. 'It's a roaring hurricane.'

'Ace of diamonds!' cried the fifth sea captain. But at that moment all the playing cards were blown off the table by the wind which came whistle-sissling in round the windows. 'Good heavens above!'

The sea captains had never known anything like this storm. The water in the harbour sploshed over the quay and licked at the doorsteps with its long tongues of foam.

'It will be tremendously rough out there,' the five sea captains thought, 'out on the Boiling Sea,' and they thought of the little madcap, sitting in the midst of it on his little boat.

'It will be lying on the bottom like a bit of crumpled lead,' they told each other and they would have taken their caps off, but the caps had already been blown off by the wind, and all five were flying through the air like black stormy petrels.

There was no need for the five sea captains to take their caps off anyway, for the *Neversink* was not sunk yet.

True, the six-bucket funnel had been blown overboard in six rattling pieces, the mast had been carried off in forty-seven splinters, the furled sail had flown away in tatters with the

hollander

driving clouds and the roof of the cabin was being banged open and shut like a lid by the churning winds, but the little boat was afloat.

It was tossed to and fro like a cork, but however hard the seething waves tried to bruise it or break it or suck it into the whirling depths, the little boat stayed whole and it stayed afloat. It was the *Neversink*.

And the crew?

The deck was swept clean, there was no one there. The cabin was full of water, the helm was spinning madly and the place behind the helm was empty. Where was the little Captain?

The little Captain was in the hold. All four of them were sitting in the hold and the hatch was firmly bolted. At the first squall of

wind the little Captain had given the order immediately: 'Get below. Batten down the hatch.'

And there they sat. Or rather, there they rolled and bowled and bashed and crashed to and fro. No one knew which arms and legs belonged to him any more, no one really knew who he was. One lump of misery had once been timid Thomas, another Marinka and the larger lump of misery was probably podgy Plum. Only the little Captain was still capable of thought.

'The coast,' thought the little Captain, 'the high, steep, hard rocky cliffs. If we're being driven towards that we shall be smashed to smithereens. Then everything will be lost, my boat, the three treasure chests and the four of us. And Scurvyboots, too.'

The little Captain listened to the wind which rushed howling along the iron hull of his boat and to the waves which sounded like thunderous hammer blows.

Hour after hour passed by. Was it day by now? Not a glimmer of light fell into the hold and it was beginning to feel close.

Then the little Captain thought of the chest, the seventh, lucky chest which they had with them in the hold. 'Shall we crawl inside?' he wondered. 'Would the chest —'

But at that moment there came a terrible groaning and cracking and creaking of iron. A shock ran through the *Neversink*, the worst they had yet known, and then the boat lay still. As still as a dead bird.

'The rocks!' That was the first thought that went through the little Captain's head when he recovered from the stunning blow. 'We have hit the cliffs. At the top, I should think.'

But could the *Neversink* possibly have been lifted *that* high by the waves?

'W-where am I?' came Marinka's voice.

'Ooh,' stammered podgy Plum, 'what a ghastly dream I had.'

'It was no dream,' said the little Captain.

'Si-si-sick . . . oooh!' timid Thomas could be heard. 'So sick . . .'

The little Captain said: 'The *Neversink* has been washed up on the rocks. We must try to open the hatch.'

But they had not the strength to do it. The screws had been bent by the might of the waves.

'Bother,' said podgy Plum.

'What do we do now?' asked Marinka.

'I want to go home!' moaned timid Thomas.

But the little Captain said: 'Wait calmly.'

And the little Captain said something else. He said: 'It's a funny thing, it feels as if we were still moving . . .'

The Floating Town

The floating town, the incredibly vast ship which crossed the Boiling Sea once a year, was not bothered by the storm. Although the slam-bang and bubble waves did their best, the ship's hull did not bend by a millimetre. And although the hurricane winds lashed and tore at roofs and chimneys, everything remained immovable.

The ship sailed calmly on, with scarcely so much as a roll.

It was a strange vessel, because the deck consisted of streets and houses, towers and windmills, a church and a tiny little white palace.

A hundred people lived in the floating town and all hundred of them slept like logs on the night of the storm.

'Brisk little blow,' they said. 'Sleep well, now!'

Only the men at the wheel had stayed up, because of course they had to steer. They steered straight for the west. When in the middle of the night they heard the sound of a heavy thud, the steersmen scarcely looked up. Just an extra-big wave, they thought.

Those few who woke up because the thud was so close to their houses, muttered: 'A storm, eh?', yawned, turned over comfortably and went on sleeping.

But next morning they rubbed their eyes in astonishment, for there, in the little square outside their windows, lay a boat. A real boat, dumped down by a huge wave.

'We've never seen the likes of that before,' cried the people of the floating town, running outside to look. What a sad little wreck! No mast, no funnel, the cabin roofless and half filled with water.

'Poor shipwrecked souls,' said one.

'Their own silly fault,' said another.

'I say,' began a third, looking pale, 'wasn't that — wasn't it yesterday evening when we heard a steam whistle? Could it be —'

'Oh yes,' said a fourth, 'that must have been this little ship. Poor —'

All of them began taking off their hats. They were not blown away, because the storm had died down.

'Look, it's called the *Neversink*,' said one.

'*Pile-of-junk* would suit it better now,' said another.

'Get some pincers,' said a third. He wanted to try to unscrew the hatch. 'There might be something inside.'

'Yes,' said a joker, 'sea water.'

The pincers did not work, because the screws were bent. But at last they managed to open the hold with a hatchet. And then the people of the floating town drew back in fright.

From the opening of the hold rose a ghost. A ghastly face, with a mop of hair, whimpering hollowly: 'Si-si-sick.'

The face vanished, there was the sound of clattering and thumping from the hold of the little boat and once again a head appeared. It shouted: 'Ahoy!'

It was not a ghost, it was a little girl who came crawling out, jumped down from the deck and asked: 'Where are we?'

The people of the floating town were speechless. At last: 'Th-then you're not drowned?' they asked.

'Of course not,' cried Marinka, and 'What did you think?' cried podgy Plum behind her.

'We are!' moaned timid Thomas, sticking his pale, ghostly face out again. 'We're shipwrecked.'

'Och, puir wee thing,' cried a woman's voice. 'Such a wee loon on a big voyage.' But then her mouth fell open wide, all their mouths fell open wide, for the little Captain had just appeared, and he too seemed to be just a little fellow.

'Maircy on us!' cried the woman. 'What kind of a wee boat is that? A bairns' boat?'

But the little fellow stood there in his big cap, feet set apart on the sloping deck, and spoke: 'I am the little Captain and this is my ship, the *Neversink*. We were overtaken by a storm and have suffered damage. Take us to your captain to discuss the matter.'

Five minutes later they were sitting in the little white palace on the floating town, in comfortable chairs with fat cushions and hot coffee and thick sandwiches on the table in front of them. All but timid Thomas, for he had been tucked up in bed with three hot water bottles and given weak tea and a biscuit.

'Well, well,' said the steward of the floating town, 'how about some more coffee? And tell us, where were you headed for?'

'The west,' said the little Captain.

'Well, that's all right!' cried the steward. 'That's the way we're going. Always westward, for years and years and years.'

'What?' asked Marinka. 'For years? Is it such a long way off?'

'Oh, lassie,' said the steward, 'we've been at least seven times round the world. Always sailing westward.'

'But — but —' podgy Plum began, 'then how can we ever — I mean we're looking — somewhere in the Wild West —'

Before podgy Plum could go on, the door opened and the captain appeared. And then another captain. For the floating town was so big that two captains were needed to command it.

'Aha,' they said. 'Welcome, castaways.'

They put out their hands. 'May we introduce ourselves? My name is Fear, and this is my brother Terror.'

The little Captain looked as if he had been struck by lightning.

'Ha ha!' they laughed. 'Don't be afraid! They're just names. That was our father's name: he was the great lord of Fear and Terror . . .'

Five Captains

Marinka was the first to be able to speak.

'Captain Fear!' she cried. 'Captain Terror!' She jumped up and flung herself on their necks, with so many kisses that the caps rolled off their heads.

'Well, well, she's not frightened,' said the captains, with scarlet cheeks.

'She's glad to have been rescued, of course,' said the steward.

'Oh no,' said podgy Plum. 'Marinka is glad that we've found them.'

'Them? What *them*?'

'You tell them, little Captain,' said podgy Plum.

The little Captain stood with his feet planted firmly apart, looked straight at the big captains and spoke: 'We were searching for the two sons of the great lord of Fear and Terror.'

Now it was their turn to stand speechless and open-mouthed.

'Yes,' the little Captain continued, 'because we have a chest for each of you. One filled with copper and one filled with red rubies.'

'W-what?'

'That's right,' the little Captain continued. 'We had seven chests for your father. But since he is no longer alive, we have had to take them round to his sons. One in the Misty East, three in the Deep South, two here in the Wild West and the last, the chest filled with good luck, we shall now have to take to your sister in the Far North.'

And the little Captain told them all about Scurvyboots the pirate, who must be released from his ghost ship, and about the adventures they had been through.

The brothers Fear and Terror looked at each other. 'Two

treasure chests,' they murmured. 'Now we can buy an engine for our tub. No one will have to row any more.'

'Row?' asked Marinka.

Podgy Plum began to laugh. 'This isn't a fairground boat, is it?' he asked.

'It's an ancient galley,' said the brothers Fear and Terror. And then they told their story. How after the death of their father they had left the country to travel west. How they had bought this vessel with the last of their money in order to be able to take the hundred faithful subjects who wanted to stay with them. How they had rowed, with fifty men at a time, on the heavy sweeps, always following the setting sun. How they had become desperate because the west never came any nearer, how in the end they had become resigned and built a town on their vessel to live in. And how they still went on rowing, in their floating town, to the west, always to the west . . .

'But now,' they cried, 'now we shall buy a big steam engine and a propeller. Then the ship will move by itself, and faster, too.'

At the end of the Boiling Sea there was another narrow channel and they passed through it into the blue ocean. On the coast lay a big port where the steam engine was built into the floating town. It was fitted with two propellers and five rudders as well.

'It's necessary,' they said, 'otherwise we shan't be able to steer the thing. You need five captains for it.'

The brothers Fear and Terror scratched their heads, but the little Captain said: 'In Xuxuxalpetl there are five sea captains. They can do it.'

That was a good idea. After the *Neversink* had been repaired, with a brand-new six-bucket funnel, a proud mast made of pine wood, a fine, strong sail and a new roof on the cabin, the floating

Hollander

town sailed away. First towards the east, back across the Boiling Sea, with the five wheels side by side in the wheelhouse manned by the brothers Fear and Terror, podgy Plum, Marinka and the little Captain. Timid Thomas did not dare.

Timid Thomas wandered all day along the streets and past the houses of the floating town and whenever clouds appeared in the sky he fled indoors.

'Come for a snack, little chap?' the women of the floating town would ask. And timid Thomas nodded, because he dared not say that he was frightened of a storm.

But no storm came during their passage. The *Neversink* could have sailed by itself instead of standing on the deck of the floating town.

So they reached Xuxuxalpetl, where the five sea captains had just started quarrelling over their cards.

'Ace of hearts — ace of spades — ace of hearts — ace of spades!' they were shouting at each other. But when they heard that all five of them could be captains of a ship at once, they cried: 'Trumps! We'll do it!'

So the floating town has been sailing across the sea from that day to this, always westward, trying to overtake the setting sun.

But the *Neversink* sailed northwards, to search for the last heir of the great lord of Fear and Terror, his youngest daughter. For the seventh chest, the chest filled with luck, was for her.

'But it's empty!' whimpered timid Thomas. 'Let's go home now.'

But the little Captain sailed straight ahead, heading for the North Pole, steady and sure behind the helm, his eyes on the horizon.

The Old Watchman

The world is so big, so big. There is more sea than land in the world. The sea is blue, or grey, but far, far to the north the sea is green. White blocks of ice float in it, as big as mountains, and it is dangerous to sail between them in a boat.

And yet a little boat was sailing over the green sea in the Far North. It had a funnel made of six buckets and the steam furnace was an upturned bathtub. At the helm a little captain stood, steering round the icebergs. In front of the furnace a podgy lad knelt, blowing up the fire. In the galley a girl stood stirring pancake mixture. On the afterdeck a shivering little boy went round with a swab and a pail. His fingers were red with cold.

The last land lies up there in the Far North. It is made of black rock and on the last point of it stands a tall lighthouse. In it lives the old watchman, making the northern lights, which shine in the polar night with red and yellow and green and sometimes with blue flames.

The old watchman is lonely and he was very pleased when he saw the little boat sailing towards him, making for the jetty to come alongside. He ran down all the stairs, the iron staircase with its six hundred and fourteen steps, and opened the lighthouse door.

'Well, well,' he said, for there were four children standing in front of him.

'I am the little Captain,' said the first, 'of the steamship *Neversink*, and this is my crew: podgy Plum, Marinka and timid Thomas.'

'Well, well,' said the old watchman again.

'May we come in?' asked the little Captain.

They walked up the six hundred and fourteen iron stairs to the little room at the top, where a stove was roaring.

The little Captain took off his cap and timid Thomas warmed his red fingers.

'Are you lost?' asked the old watchman.

'No,' said the little Captain, 'we're on a search.'

'For polar bears?' asked the old watchman. 'Or for whales?'

'For a noble lady,' said the little Captain.

'Well, well.'

'Have you heard of her?' asked the little Captain.

The old watchman scratched his grey head. 'The Noble Lady of the Far North lives in the ice citadel on top of the slippery Slitherberg,' he said. 'What do you want with her?'

'We've got a present for her,' said the little Captain. 'A chest full of good luck.'

The old watchman did not laugh. 'Ah,' he said, 'that would do her good. The Noble Lady of the Far North is a sad lady. But a chest! You'll never get a chest up the slippery Slitherberg. You won't be able to get up it yourselves. No one can get up.'

'Perhaps the Noble Lady would come down?' asked the little Captain.

The old watchman shook his head. 'Never,' he said.

'We'll go and try, all the same,' said the little Captain. 'It's for the pirate Scurvyboots.'

'Is he in the chest?' asked the watchman anxiously.

'No,' said the little Captain. 'The pirate Scurvyboots is sailing round on his ghost ship with his hands fixed to the wheel by a spell. It's a punishment, because he stole the seven chests full of treasure. We've taken six chests back and one of Scurvyboots' hands is already free. The seventh chest is for the Noble Lady. She's the daughter of the great lord of Fear and Terror, for whom the treasure was meant.'

The old watchman scratched his grey head again. 'Scurvy-boots,' he muttered, 'that's another sorry business.'

The little Captain asked: 'Where does the ice castle lie?'

'No!' cried timid Thomas suddenly. He sat shivering beside the hot stove.

'He's so cold,' said Marinka. 'Have you got a pullover for him?'

'I've got pullovers for you all,' said the old watchman. 'I've got furry suits for you. If you are really going to the icy citadel on the slippery Slitherberg you will have to wear polar outfits.'

Polar outfits are the warmest clothes in the world, with fur on the inside. Podgy Plum was as round as a barrel when he put his on and timid Thomas looked like an Eskimo. Marinka thought the colour was dull and the little Captain put his cap on top of his fur hood. It fitted properly at last. The old watchman showed them the way to go. 'It's three days' sail,' he said. 'Look out for icebergs and for polar bears.'

The little Captain thanked him and was about to set off down the six hundred and fourteen iron steps again, but the old watchman said: 'I have something else for you.'

From a little box he took two sticks with a knob on the end and gave them to the little Captain. 'These are signal rockets,' he said. 'This one gives a green light — set it off if things are going well. But this one gives a red light — set it off if you are in danger. Farewell!'

A quarter of an hour later the steam whistle on the *Neversink* shrilled until it echoed from the icebergs and with a foaming wake, the brave little boat sailed off across the green sea. Further, ever further towards the Far North, in the direction of the white ice castle on the slippery Slitherberg, which no one, since the lady, had yet been able to climb.

Northern Lights

After three days' sailing the *Neversink* was so far to the north that the sun could only be seen suspended in the distance like a red balloon, just above the horizon. The light was dim, as if it were evening all day long, and in that half light the icebergs looked ghostly. Only towards midnight did the red sun dip behind the horizon and complete darkness fall. It was a short night. Then the little Captain stopped the *Neversink*, and the four children went off to sleep in their hammocks.

They had strange dreams.

The little Captain dreamed of a mysteriously beautiful woman in a mysteriously beautiful castle. She was very sweet and very sad.

Podgy Plum dreamed of polar bears chasing him, panting and snuffling. He ran away, but the ground was so slippery that he never got any further.

Marinka dreamed of a rumbustious pirate flying through the air like a bird, but he had no wings.

Timid Thomas dreamed of green light, which glittered so dazzlingly in his eyes that it woke him up. How can that be? thought Thomas. It's pitch dark, isn't it?

He slipped out of his hammock and climbed sleepily through the hatch on deck. The night was still as death, the Pole Star shining almost directly above timid Thomas's head.

Then, suddenly, a strange light flickered across the sky. Green light, yellow light, red light. It swelled and died like candlelight, shaping strange, magical figures, so that timid Thomas could only think that his dream was still going on.

He stared open-mouthed at the icebergs, in which all the

colours were dazzlingly reflected, and suddenly he saw the White Citadel straight ahead. High on a mountain top, with sides as smooth as glass, the citadel lay sparkling in the enchanted light. Walls, towers, pinnacles and battlements, and even the doors, were made of clear ice.

'There!' cried timid Thomas. 'There, there!' He pointed with both hands, stretching forward as far as possible over the iron railing.

That was how they found him next morning, stiff as a sleepwalker.

Timid Thomas was woken up with hot coffee. 'Dream,' he stammered, 'lovely dream.' But when he told them about the Citadel, Marinka said: 'It must be another mirage.'

The little Captain shook his head. 'Northern lights,' he said. 'They are real,' and he steered the *Neversink* in the direction towards which timid Thomas had been pointing.

The passage between the icebergs grew narrower and narrower, and the *Neversink* might easily have been crushed. But the little Captain sailed boldly on, blowing the steam whistle as he went. 'To scare off the polar bears,' he said.

'P-p-polar b-b-b-?' Timid Thomas could not even get the word to cross his lips, but he was shuddering with cold, too.

'I haven't seen a single one yet,' said podgy Plum calmly.

'Full speed ahead!' cried the little Captain suddenly.

They had entered a narrow channel and it looked as if the two icebergs were drifting closer and closer to each other. The fairway was shrinking rapidly.

'Double power!' cried the little Captain. 'Keep stoking up that furnace!'

Podgy Plum blew out his cheeks until he was as red as a lobster, Marinka rowed with the cooking spoon, timid Thomas

hollander

with the swab, but the fairway grew narrower and narrower.

'Help!' screamed timid Thomas. 'We shall be crushed.'

The little Captain tugged at the steam whistle.

'Help!' shrieked timid Thomas. 'We shall be eaten up.'

But there were no polar bears to be seen.

There was a block of ice — a huge block of ice which had been wobbling on the slope of the iceberg for years and now lost its balance, because of the vibrant shriek of the steam whistle. Rumblecumtumble, down it shot, making straight for the little boat.

But — perhaps the good luck chest on board had something to do with it — at the last moment the block turned aside and, instead of landing with a crash on the *Neversink*, it landed with a splash in the water behind the *Neversink*. It made an enormous wave and just as the little boat was about to be stuck fast between the walls of ice it was picked up by the wave and thrust forward into a patch of open sea.

The little Captain removed his cap.

Podgy Plum stayed where he was, kneeling in front of the furnace.

Marinka began to giggle: the whole of her fur jacket was soaked from the splash, she cried.

Timid Thomas stuck his head out of the hold and shouted: 'There, there, there!'

They all looked. There lay the White Citadel.

Thomas's dream had not been a dream. The slippery Slitherberg was really there, rising out of the green sea, cold, hard and shiny, like a looking-glass. The White Citadel, right at the top, looked as far out of reach as the moon.

The Signal Rocket

Three times the *Neversink* sailed slowly round the slippery Slitherberg. But the slopes were all made of ice. Not a bough, not a brick, not a boulder stuck out anywhere, there were no stairs to be seen, nor even a rope — everything was of the slipperiest ice, without a single handhold.

The little Captain sounded the steam whistle from time to time, but no window, no doorway in the White Citadel opened and nobody appeared on the battlements. The great doors remained tight shut; there was not a sign of life to be seen.

'I bet the Noble Lady is frozen fast to her chair,' said podgy Plum.

'She may not even be at home,' said Marinka.

But the little Captain turned off the engine and let the *Neversink* drift gently towards the foot of the mountain.

There was no mooring jetty, but the foot of the mountain was flat. You could walk a little way, to the beginning of the smooth slope.

The little Captain cast anchor and podgy Plum jumped ashore. 'There seems to be a path here,' he cried. 'It runs right the way round the mountain!'

Podgy Plum began to run straight for the slope, but he got no further than a step or two. Then he slipped backwards like a struggling seal in his thick Eskimo clothes. 'No good!' he cried.

But the little Captain brought the seventh chest up from the hold of the *Neversink*, the last chest they had to deliver, the chest full of luck. He set it down on shore.

'And now?' asked Marinka.

'It's got to go up,' said the little Captain.

Marinka thought it was ridiculous. 'The thing is empty,' she

said. 'Leave it here, little Captain, won't that do?'

'No,' said the little Captain. 'It has to go to the Noble Lady in the White Citadel. Up there.'

'An empty chest!' Podgy Plum thought it was crazy, too. 'Let's turn back again,' he said. 'I bet you there's not a soul living in the whole Citadel, let alone a sorrowful lady. Bah!'

The little Captain did not answer. The little Captain stooped and began to push the chest forward like a sledge across the ice. He began to push it up the slope and his feet began to slip. Skid-skid on the smooth ice — he got no higher, but he went on pushing and pushing.

Marinka could not bear to watch any longer. She ran across to him and pushed as well, pushing the little Captain himself from behind. 'I can't leave him in the lurch now,' she thought, 'even if it's all mad.'

The chest moved up a little.

Podgy Plum looked at their struggling legs, skid-skid on the smooth ice. 'The little Captain,' he thought, 'the little Captain has gone round the bend.' But even as he thought, podgy Plum took a run, bumped into Marinka so that she jerked forward, and he began to push too, skid-skid over the smooth ice.

The chest moved up a little further.

'Timid Thomas,' called Plum, 'help us!'

But timid Thomas was still on the *Neversink*. He did not dare to come ashore.

'Come on, Thomas!' cried podgy Plum. 'Don't be so scared. There's no danger here!'

Skid-skid went their feet over the ice and finally podgy Plum heard a panting and snuffling behind him. Timid Thomas had found enough courage, after all, he thought to himself.

'Forward, shove!'

But instead of hands on his back, podgy Plum felt a wet nose on his neck.

He looked round.

It was not timid Thomas. It was a polar bear. A live one.

Podgy Plum gave a yell. He did the only thing he could do: he redoubled his efforts and ran so hard on his skidding feet that Marinka, the little Captain and the lucky chest rose another two and a half metres up the slope.

'Well done, Plum!' shouted Marinka, and she looked around too. 'A polar bear!' yelled Marinka, and she and the little Captain also redoubled their efforts, which took them another whole metre further up.

The polar bear was just unable to reach them.

There they were, a little way up the smooth slope of the slippery Slitherberg, running and skidding and running for their lives. It was like a nightmare in which you cannot move a step forward. How long could they keep it up?

'Timid Thomas!' they screamed. 'Chase him away!'

As if timid Thomas would dare! Pale as a corpse, he stood

watching, as if nailed to the deck of the *Neversink*, too frightened even to scream.

But then, suddenly, timid Thomas thought of the two signal rockets which the old watchman on the lighthouse had given them. The green one if things were going well and the red for an emergency. And suddenly timid Thomas went into action. Trembling, quaking and quivering, he went looking for the sticks with the knobs on, and found them at last in the cabin. 'I need the red one, I need the red one,' babbled Thomas. 'This one!' He stuck the stick in a bottle on the afterdeck, lit a match, and another, and another, until at last he was holding a flickering flame to the fuse.

Hissing, the rocket shot up into the dusky polar night and illuminated the icy scene of the slopes of the slippery Slitherberg in a fierce light.

Green light.

Timid Thomas had set off the wrong rocket.

He had used the last match.

The old watchman, who saw the light from his distant lighthouse, murmured contentedly: 'Aha, so everything is all right.'

But there was someone else who noticed the safe, green colour with satisfaction. Someone at sea . . .

The Lucky Chest

For weeks and weeks on end the pirate Scurvyboots had been steering his ghost ship with only one hand. His other hand had been released from the spell and he did not dare to touch the helm with his free hand again. The wind had driven his ship towards the Far North and Scurvyboots was navigating with great difficulty among the icebergs, always with only one hand on the wheel.

'That's luck!' thought the pirate, when the green light of a rocket flashed before his eyes in the dusk. 'There's a safe stretch of open water.'

He made straight for it at full speed.

'For here and yonder!' shouted the pirate, and then gripped the wheel in both hands, for suddenly the slippery Slitherberg reared up ahead of him. He wrenched fiercely at the wheel, but it was too late. With a deafening crash his wooden ship rammed the iceberg, close to the place where the *Neversink* lay. Masts under full sail snapped like reeds and the bows finished up amidships, but the steering wheel was finally torn off and sailed, with the pirate held fast to it by magic, at full speed through the air.

'Help! A shipwreck!' yelled timid Thomas from the deck of the *Neversink*.

The little Captain, Marinka and podgy Plum, who were still trying to make their way further up the icy slope with skidding feet, drew breath in relief. For the polar bear, which had been waiting, jaws agape, for them to slip down again, fled from the noise of the shipwreck in one great leap.

The little Captain had just been thinking that they would have to try to crawl inside the lucky chest before the polar bear snapped them up. He had already opened the lid, but now it was no longer necessary.

Or was it?

A lucky chest is not a lucky chest for nothing, for lo and behold: the pirate Scurvyboots, who came sailing through the air at that very moment, plumped straight into it. As if into open jaws, with the wheel still in his hands, and still at full speed. At such speed that the chest, with the pirate inside, and the little Captain, Marinka and podgy Plum behind it, zoomed up the slopes of the slippery Slitherberg and shot straight in through the icy doors of the White Citadel.

Timid Thomas was left behind alone, down on the deck of the *Neversink*, and timid Thomas at once began to cry because they had left him in the lurch, all alone in the dark polar night, with polar bears lying in wait for him and an abandoned ghost ship beside him. 'Boo-hoo!' howled timid Thomas.

'*Hoo*!' The sound came back from the White Citadel. But it was not the voice of timid Thomas. It was the voice of the sorrowful lady.

Dazed and bemused, the three children looked round, but there was no one to be seen. They could see only walls, made of ice. A ceiling, made of ice. Arches, pillars, buttresses, all ice. Tables, chairs, benches, all of ice. And at the end of the hall a wide staircase, of hard, smooth, glistening ice.

'Chilly,' said Marinka.

'Cool and cold,' said podgy Plum.

'We must look for her,' said the little Captain.

The pirate Scurvyboots said nothing. He saw nothing, either. The pirate Scurvyboots lay unconscious in the chest.

'He must go away,' said Marinka.

'He doesn't belong here,' said podgy Plum

But the little Captain shut the lid.

And at that moment, from the top of the stairs, they heard a sad song:

'I am the Lady of the North,
but all the knights who come to woo
by cold and ice are driven forth
and splash back in the sea, boo-hoo!
And now I think I'll never see
a courtier come to rescue me.
Boo-hoo, oo-hoo, how smooth the ice!
Boo-hoo, oo-hoo, it would be nice
to have a path: *one* would suffice!'

Slowly she came down the stairs, the sad lady, with a flickering candle in her hand. She looked like a ghost.

'Ahoy,' said the little Captain.

Giving no answer, she descended the icy stairs without slipping once and came slowly towards them. She might have been sleep-walking.

'Ah, why?' she sang. 'It always seems,
saviours come only in my dreams.'

'It's not a dream!' Marinka cried in a clear voice. 'We're real!'

But the little Captain took the Noble Lady by the hand and led her towards the chest.

'Sorrowful lady,' he said, 'we have brought this with us. It is the seventh chest, and filled with luck. It is for you.'

'This is really too silly for words,' cried podgy Plum. 'You can't do that, little Captain, after all it's got —'

Podgy Plum got no further.

With a crash the lid flew open, and snorting as if he had risen from the water, Scurvyboots the pirate rose up from the chest. 'For here and yonder!' he bellowed, still clutching the wheel of his ghost ship. 'Astern! Full speed astern. We are sinking! We —'

Then he saw the Noble Lady, and the Noble Lady saw him.

They gazed deep into one another's eyes and fell in love at a stroke, the pirate and the Noble Lady, and then the wheel clattered to the ground from his hands, and the candle from hers.

Scurvyboots was released from the spell.

The Noble Lady of the Far North had found her luck.

A Party in the Citadel

The White Citadel was lighted with a thousand candles and wooden steps ran from the doors to the foot of the slippery Slitherberg. Seventy-two steps, made out of the wrecked wood of the ghost ship. The *Neversink* was moored to the bottom-most step, but there was another ship there too. A gigantic ship. The floating town.

With its five sea captains, the floating town had sailed around the world, from the Wild West past the Deep South and the Misty East, until it arrived here in the Far North. All the sons of the great lord of Fear and Terror had come along, and now they were giving a party, up there in the White Citadel. For the marriage of their sister to Scurvyboots, who was no longer a pirate, was being celebrated, and she was now known as the Joyful Lady

'Yoho!' cried Lord Fear.

'Och aye!' cried Lord Terror.

'Rumblecumtumble hurrah!' cried Borrow and Morrow.

'Pling!' went Allmysorrow.

'Yes, yes, well,' even the lord of Quake and Quiver nodded. He was sitting on a chair. He was not dancing. The ice floor was too slippery for him.

'Great heavens above!' thundered the five sea captains, going off to play cards happily in a corner.

Podgy Plum and Marinka twirled, slipping and sliding, through the hall and timid Thomas had dressed up as a polar bear so that he wouldn't need to be frightened of anyone.

In the end they all danced round the bridal pair, who sat in the middle, on the lucky chest.

'Hurrah!' came the shouts.

'Hurrah for the little Captain!' they shouted. 'The little Captain has saved us all!'

They wanted to drink to him, but where was the little Captain? Not in the ballroom, not in the corridors, not in the cellar, not upstairs.

The little Captain was standing outside, looking at the stars. At the Pole Star above his head, at the Great Bear, at the silvery Swan and at the red eye of the Bull. At the seven twinkling Pleiades, at the Whale and at the Dragon's swishing tail.

'Little Captain,' called the Noble Lady, 'what are you doing out there?'

'Noble Lady,' the little Captain answered, 'I am seeing where I have to go.'

'Won't you stay with us?' the lady asked. 'I will be your mother.'

'Do, do!' cried Scurvyboots, beaming. 'I'll be your father.'

But the little Captain shook his head.

'Where is your home then, little Captain?' asked the lady.

The little Captain stretched out his arm and pointed. Towards the *Neversink*? Towards the wide sea? Or to a place somewhere in the world which no one knew? None of them dared to ask.

Next morning the *Neversink* set sail, while everyone in the Citadel waved goodbye. The whistle blew, podgy Plum stoked the furnace, Marinka put butter in the frying pan, timid Thomas dipped his swabs in the clean water and the little Captain stood behind the wheel, legs astride, his eyes on the horizon.

They sailed without stopping, by the light of the red sun-balloon by day, and by the blue, yellow and green flames of the northern lights at night.

They put in when they reached the old watchman in the lighthouse, to return their North Polar clothes, and after that it was straight ahead for home. Home for Marinka, podgy Plum and timid Thomas. But for the little Captain?

'You can come and live with us,' said Marinka.

'With us too!' cried podgy Plum.

'And I-I will ask my mother,' stammered timid Thomas.

But the little Captain shook his head.

Once again a party was held in the little village among the dunes, because the children had returned safely in the *Neversink*.

hollander

'Well, little Captain, here you are again!' said old Salty. 'I'll drink a beer to that. Your health! Will you come and live with me?'

But the little Captain shook his head. Then he made a speech.

'Marinka,' he said, 'you were the bravest, because you sailed into the harbour of the Misty East in the good luck chest.

'Podgy Plum,' he said, 'you were the strongest, because you kept the *Neversink* going by always stoking up the fire.

'Timid Thomas,' he said, 'you were the best.'

Thomas blinked.

'You are timid, Thomas,' said the little Captain, 'but thanks to your *helphelphelp* tracks in the sand we found the sons in the south. And thanks to your choosing the wrong signal light, Scurvyboots landed in the good-luck chest.'

Timid Thomas quivered, but not with fear.

'That's how the world goes,' said the little Captain, 'but reason has nothing to do with it,' and he went outside, into the bright, starry night.

Next morning the *Neversink* had sailed away. The little Captain had left without a blast from the whistle and with the engine running softly, to sail the wide blue sea. Had he gone to seek the place he came from, or was the *Neversink* his only home?

If that is true, you may see him sailing past one day, when you are standing on the beach. The *Neversink* is a small boat and the little Captain is always at the helm, steady and sure, his eyes fixed on the horizon.